COOKING HEALTHY

COOKING WITH FRUITS AND VEGETABLES

BY CLAIRE LLEWELLYN
WITH RECIPES BY CLARE O'SHEA

rosen publishing's
rosen central

New York

Published in 2012 by The Rosen Publishing Group Inc.
29 East 21st Street, New York, NY 10010

Copyright © 2012 Wayland/
The Rosen Publishing Group, Inc.

First Edition

Commissioning Editor: Jennifer Sanderson
Designer: www.rawshock.co.uk
Photographer: Andy Crawford
Illustrator: Ian Thompson
Hand Model: Camilla Lloyd
Proofreader and Indexer: Susie Brooks
Food Consultant: Clare O'Shea

Library of Congress Cataloging-in-Publication Data

Llewellyn, Claire.
Cooking with fruits and vegetables / Claire Llewellyn, Clare O'Shea.
    p. cm. -- (Cooking healthy)
Includes index.
ISBN 978-1-4488-4844-7 (library binding)
1. Cooking (Fruit)--Juvenile literature. 2. Cooking (Vegetables)--Juvenile literature. 3. Cookbooks. I. O'Shea, Clare. II. Title.
TX811.L55 2012
641.3'4--dc22

                              2010039333

Manufactured in China
CPSIA Compliance Information: Batch #S11YA:
For Further Information contact Rosen Publishing, New York, New York at 1-800-237-9932

Photographs:
All photography by Andy Crawford, except Tomas del Amo/Alamy: 10; Dorling Kindersley/Getty Images: 19T; Frank Herholdt/Getty Images: 43; Gary Holscher/AgStock Images/Corbis: 31; iStockphoto: 6, 23T; Ron Levine/Getty Images: 4; Andrew Linscott/Alamy: 39; Stuart O'Sullivan/Getty Images: 35; Thomas Weightman/Alamy: 15;

Note:
In preparation of this book, all due care has been exercised with regard to the advice, activities, and techniques depicted. The publishers regret that they can accept no liability for any loss or injury sustained. Always follow manufacturers' advice when using kitchen appliances and kitchen equipment.

Contents

Plants and a Balanced Diet

Fruit and vegetables are the edible parts of plants. There is an enormous variety of fruit, from apples and plums to pumpkins and peppers. Vegetables include carrots, cauliflower, onions, and potatoes.

Growing Fruit and Vegetables

Most of the fruit and vegetables that people buy in supermarkets are grown on farms and market gardens. Some farmers grow organic produce that has not been sprayed with pesticides and has been grown using only natural fertilizers. Many varieties of both fruit and vegetables are grown locally, according to the season, while others are imported from warmer countries. Some people grow their fruit and vegetables in their own gardens.

A Vegetarian Diet

Many people choose not to eat meat or fish. Instead they rely on dairy foods and plants, such as legumes, for their protein. A vegetarian diet is a healthy choice so long as it includes plenty of beans, nuts, and seeds. These foods contain proteins but, unlike the proteins in meat or fish, they must be combined with one another to provide a complete form of protein. For example, baked beans with toast provide complete protein, because they combine navy beans (a legume) with wheat (a seed grain).

A Healthy Diet

The food we eat, or our diet, is an important part of a healthy lifestyle. There are five main food groups that contain different nutrients that work together to keep the body healthy. These groups are often shown on a "food plate," where you can see the proportions in which they should be eaten (see page 5).

Added to these food groups is water. We need about six to eight glasses of water each day to keep our bodies healthy.

This farm worker is harvesting a field of organic kale. Organic produce is grown without the use of pesticides and artificial fertilizers.

The Food Plate

Fruit and vegetables: Full of vitamins and minerals, these foods protect our body and reduce the risk of heart disease, stroke, and some cancers. The fiber in them helps to bulk up our food and keep our digestive system healthy. Fruit and vegetables are low in fat so they fill us up without unnecessary calories.

Carbohydrates: These provide us with energy. Starchy carbohydrates, which include grains and cereals, should make up about 30 percent of the food we eat. Starchy carbohydrates are an important source of energy for sportsmen and women because they release the energy slowly, keeping them going for longer.

FRUIT AND VEGETABLES

CARBOHYDRATES

PROTEIN

FATS

MILK AND DAIRY

Protein: This builds and repairs our bones, muscles, skin, hair, and body tissues. Meat, fish, eggs, and legumes, which provide body-building proteins, should make up about 15 percent of our daily diet.

Fats: These keep us warm and can also be stored in the body for energy. Foods that are high in saturated fats (fats from animal sources) or sugar, such as cakes, cookies, and chips, should be eaten only in small amounts (about 8 percent of our total diet). Fats found in oily fish, olives, and nuts and seeds are called unsaturated fats. Saturated fats are linked to an increased risk of heart disease. Eating unsaturated fats is a healthier alternative.

Dairy: Dairy products include milk, butter, yogurt, and cheese. They are packed with nutrients, such as calcium, magnesium, Vitamin K, zinc, and protein, and help to build strong bones and teeth. Yogurt is full of good bacteria and improves our immune system and digestive health. It is best to eat cheese in moderation because it is high in fat.

FOOD FACTS

Doctors advise us to eat at least five portions of fruit and vegetables each day. For example, one portion is:
7 cherry tomatoes
2-inch (5-centimeter) piece of cucumber

Half a red bell pepper
3 heaping tablespoons of cooked vegetables
1 apple
1 orange
5 fl. oz. (150 ml) fresh fruit juice

Looking at Vegetables

From savory onions to sweet roasted parsnips, vegetables add goodness and flavor to our diet. Once served only as an accompaniment, they are now used to make meals in their own right, satisfying vegetarians and meat-eaters alike.

Eating Vegetables

There are so many kinds of vegetables available that they provide a huge variety of vitamins and minerals. They can be eaten raw in salads or cooked in soups, stuffed or baked as a meal in themselves, or added to stews, risottos, pasta, and pizza. They also make tasty side dishes to main courses.

The nutrients in vegetables are easily destroyed by cooking, so you should try to eat some of them raw. If you are boiling them, cook them for as short a time as possible in very little liquid. This is called blanching. Vegetables can also be steamed, roasted, fried, barbecued, broiled, or stir-fried.

Processing Vegetables

After harvesting, vegetables may be frozen, dried, canned, made into sauces, or added to all kinds of prepared meals, such as soups and broths. Fresh vegetables can be preserved by boiling them with vinegar, sugar, spices, and fruit. This produces tasty pickles and chutneys and other kinds of relishes.

Processing vegetables allows us to eat them all year round, even when they are out of season. For example, canned tomatoes are useful in the winter, when fresh tomatoes have less flavor.

Fresh peas are very tender but quickly turn hard and starchy. If they are frozen within hours of picking, they stay soft and sweet.

FOOD FACTS

Many plants are grown for their seeds, which are dried in order to preserve them. They are known as legumes and include lentils, chickpeas, kidney beans, navy beans, and lima beans.

Vegetable Types

Vegetable fruits: These fleshy, seed-bearing fruits are classed as vegetables because they taste less sweet than other fruits. They include eggplant, zucchini, peppers, squashes, cucumbers, and tomatoes.

Leaves: These are the edible leaves of a plant and include cabbage, lettuce, spinach, and bok choi.

Flowers: These are the edible flowers of a plant, for instance, cauliflower and broccoli.

Fungi: Edible fungi are known as mushrooms. There are many varieties, including oyster, shiitake, chestnut, and button.

Bulbs: These are layered, segmented vegetables that grow just below the surface of the ground and produce leafy shoots. They include onions, shallots, garlic, green onions, and leeks.

Tubers: These are vegetables that grow under the ground on the root of a plant. They include potatoes, sweet potatoes, yams, and Jerusalem artichokes.

Roots: These are the swollen root of a plant and include carrots, turnips, beets, swedes, radishes, parsnips, and celeriacs.

Seeds: The seeds and sometimes the pods of plants such as fava beans, green beans, and peas are eaten.

Stems: These are the stalks of a plant. They include asparagus, celery, and kohlrabi.

Looking at Fruits

For many people, sweet fruit is irresistible and includes some of the best-tasting foods that nature can provide. From crunchy green apples to soft white peaches, fruit provides us with fabulous flavors, which cannot be replaced by any other foods.

Eating Fruit

Most fruits, such as apples, bananas, tangerines, and grapes, are good for snacking and can be eaten raw. Alternatively, they can be sliced over breakfast cereals or added to salads. Fruit is used in dozens of desserts, including tarts, pies, crumbles, flans, jellies, ice creams, sorbets, mousses, and trifles. It can also be squeezed or blended to make juices, smoothies, and other drinks. Some fruits are traditionally served with meat; think of roast pork with apple sauce, ham and pineapple, and turkey with cranberry sauce. The fruit contrasts with the richness of the meat and helps our body to digest it. Many fruits, such as berries and tropical fruits, make the perfect end to a meal. It is healthiest to eat them as they are, without fatty whipped cream, ice cream, or custard.

In summer, when fruits are plentiful, they can be boiled with sugar to make preserves and jellies. In winter, bitter oranges can be made into marmalade.

Dried apricots make a delicious and nutritious snack—in fact, they have a much greater nutritional value than fresh apricots because their content is so concentrated. They contain fiber, vitamins, and minerals, such as iron.

Processing Fruit

Fruit is delicious when it is fresh, but it can also be preserved. Dried fruit, such as raisins, currants, prunes, and apricots, can be added to muesli or used in scones, tea loaves, and cakes. Dried fruit can also be soaked in water and cooked until it is soft. Fruit can be canned, frozen, preserved in jellies and marmalades, bottled in syrup, or made into sauces. Frozen fruit retains more of its nutrients than canned fruit.

Fruit Groups

Tropical fruits: This diverse group includes fruits that grow in the warmest parts of the world. Bananas, mangoes, pineapples, papayas, passion fruit, and kiwi fruit are all tropical fruits.

Orchard fruits: These grow on fruit trees on farms and in market gardens. They include apples, pears, plums, cherries, apricots, and peaches.

Citrus fruits: These are juicy fruits covered in a thick peel that grow on trees and shrubs in subtropical climates. They include oranges, lemons, limes, grapefruit, and tangerines.

Berries and currants: Small, soft, juicy berries are grown on bushes or smaller plants. They include strawberries, raspberries, loganberries, black currants, red currants, and blackberries.

FOOD FACTS

Kiwi fruit contain more Vitamin C than most citrus fruits. They also contain a lot of fiber, which helps the intestines to work properly.

Salad Vegetables

Served as a appetizer, a side dish, or a main course, salads are colorful, delicious, and nutritious. Almost any fresh vegetable can be included, according to taste and the season.

Why Eat Salads?

Salads are a very healthy choice because raw vegetables are bursting with goodness. Some of the vitamins and minerals that these foods contain are lost in cooking. Salad is the perfect food for a hot summer's day, although different ingredients, such as cabbage and carrots, can create tasty winter salads—a change from heavier winter meals. Salads are flexible, too. You can transform a salad into a main course by adding fish, eggs, or pasta. Salads are simple because many of them involve no cooking!

FOOD FACTS

Eating a side salad with each meal is an easy way to reach your five portions of fruit and vegetables a day. For maximum benefit, choose salad ingredients of different colors—green spinach, yellow and orange bell peppers, red tomatoes—because they contain different nutrients.

Salads are healthy and delicious. All that chewing makes us eat more slowly, and helps us to feel "full"!

Salads Around the World

There are dozens of salad recipes and some of them are specific to certain countries or regions. Many of these originated in hot places, where cold food is preferred during the heat of the day. Salade niçoise, which originated in the south of France, combines lettuce, cold potatoes, green beans, tomatoes, anchovies, hard-boiled eggs, and parsley. Taboulleh, a refreshing salad eaten throughout the Middle East, is made of bulgar wheat mixed with lots of lemon juice, mint, and parsley, along with cucumber, tomato, and green onion. In a Greek salad, tangy feta cheese is combined with tomato, cucumber, and olives. The world-famous Caesar salad includes crisp lettuce leaves served with grated cheese, crispy croutons, and a garlic dressing.

Choosing and Storing Salad Vegetables

Avoid pre-prepared bagged salads, which are less fresh than those prepared at home. Look for vegetables that are firm and fresh, rejecting any that are limp or soft. Store salad ingredients in the vegetable drawer in your refrigerator for up to one week.

Salad Dressings

Many salads are served with a sauce, which is called a dressing. Popular salad dressings include vinaigrette, which is widely eaten throughout the world but particularly in southern Europe. In Scandinavia and Eastern Europe, dressings—for example, on potato salad—are often based on mayonnaise, yogurt, or sour cream and are sometimes mixed with blue cheese for a rich, creamy dressing.

Basic Vinaigrette

MAKES: ⅔ CUP (160ML) **PREPARATION TIME: 5 MINUTES** **COOKING TIME: NO COOKING**

This dressing will work with any salad.

Ingredients
½ cup (120 ml) extra virgin olive oil
2 tablespoons vinegar
1 teaspoon lemon juice
salt and pepper

1. Whisk all the ingredients together in a bowl.

2. Add salt and pepper to taste.

3. If not using immediately, pour the dressing into a container and shake well before using.

COOK'S TIP

You can add a teaspoon of Dijon mustard if you like.

Salade Niçoise

This salad originated in the south of France. It makes a hearty main meal, perfect for a warm summer's day.

Ingredients
1 lb. (450 g) new potatoes,
12 oz. (340 g) thin green beans,
  cut in half
1 small fennel bulb, thinly sliced
1 teaspoon extra virgin olive oil
lettuce leaves
12 baby plum tomatoes, cut in half
3 hard-boiled eggs, quartered
12 black olives, without pits

For the dressing
2 oz. (50 g) can anchovy fillets,
  drained
1 small garlic clove, peeled
2 teaspoons Dijon mustard
1 teaspoon lemon juice
4 teaspoons extra virgin olive oil

1. Boil water for the potatoes in a saucepan. When the water is boiling, add the potatoes and cook them for about 15 minutes, until tender. Add the beans after 10 minutes.

2. Drain the potatoes and the beans in a colander and rinse under cold running water.

3. Cut the potatoes in half and put them and the beans in a large mixing bowl. Add the fennel.

4. To make the salad dressing, put three of the anchovy fillets and the garlic into a blender. Blend them to make a smooth purée.

5. Add the mustard, lemon juice, and oil and process until smooth.

6. Pour the dressing over the vegetables in the bowl and stir well to mix.

7. Put a layer of lettuce leaves on each one of four plates. Divide the potato mixture among them.

8. Arrange the tomatoes and egg quarters around the edge of each plate. Scatter the olives over the salad.

9. Add the remaining anchovies, dividing them equally among each plate of salad. Serve immediately.

COOK'S TIP

Sprinkle some toasted pine nuts or sesame seeds over the top of the salad for extra crunch and flavor and protein.

Summer Couscous Salad

SERVES: 4	PREPARATION TIME: 20 MINUTES	COOKING TIME: NO COOKING

This salad is a perfect accompaniment to food cooked on a barbecue.

Ingredients
1½ cups (250 g) couscous
20 cherry tomatoes, quartered
1 small red onion, peeled and
  finely chopped
4 in. (10 cm) piece of cucumber,
  chopped
1 large carrot, peeled and grated
2 tablespoons fresh cilantro,
  chopped
salt and pepper

For the dressing
¼ teaspoon ground cumin
1 small garlic clove, peeled and
finely chopped
1 tablespoon lemon juice
3 tablespoons olive oil

1. Put the couscous into a bowl and pour over enough boiling water to cover it completely. Stir well and leave it to soak for about 15–20 minutes.

2. In the meantime, make the dressing by whisking together the cumin, garlic, lemon juice, and oil in a small bowl.

3. When the couscous is ready, add the tomatoes, onion, cucumber, carrot, and cilantro.

4. Pour the dressing over the salad, season, and mix well.

Caesar Salad

SERVES: 2–4	PREPARATION TIME: 20 MINUTES	COOKING TIME: 10 MINUTES

This salad is often served with a broiled breast of chicken to make chicken Caesar salad.

Ingredients
1 garlic clove, peeled and
  crushed
1 tablespoon olive oil
12 thin slices French bread,
  cut into slices
1 firm romaine lettuce,
  torn into bite-
  sized pieces
1 small Belgian
  endive head,
  sliced
4 celery sticks,
  sliced
1 oz. (30 g) Parmesan,
  finely sliced

For the dressing
1 teaspoon Dijon mustard
3 tablespoons olive oil
2 teaspoons white vinegar
2 teaspoons natural yogurt
large pinch superfine sugar
½ teaspoon Worcestershire sauce
salt and pepper

1. Preheat the oven to 400°F (200°C).

2. Combine the garlic and olive oil.

3. To make croutons, brush one side of each slice of bread with the garlic oil. Bake for 10 minutes until crisp. Cut the slices into cubes.

4. Whisk together all the dressing ingredients and season to taste.

5. Put the lettuce, endive, and celery in a bowl and pour half of the dressing on top. Toss the salad.

6. Divide the salad into 2 or 4 portions. Drizzle the remaining dressing over it, scatter the cheese on top, and add the croutons to serve.

Roots and Tubers

Root vegetables and tubers sustain us during the colder seasons, when they add heartiness and sweetness to our meals and help to keep us warm. They include carrots, beets, parsnips, swedes, celeriac, radishes, and different kinds of potatoes.

What Are Roots and Tubers?

Most plants have thin, fibrous roots, which they use to cling to the soil and to take in water. Some plants, however, such as carrots and parsnips, use their roots in another way: to store food that will sustain the plant in the following year. The roots on these plants become fat as they swell up with sugar, starch, and other carbohydrates. The roots give us energy, vitamins, and minerals while being low in fat. Tubers, such as potatoes, sweet potatoes, and Jerusalem artichokes, are slightly different. They are swollen pieces of stem that grow among the roots of a plant.

Where Are They Eaten?

Root vegetables are eaten all over the world. In many places they are staple foods. For example, in parts of Africa, a root vegetable called cassava

is just as important as grains. In Russia, root vegetables are used in a salad that combines a mixture of diced, cooked vegetables, bound together with mayonnaise. In cool, temperate places, potatoes are a staple food. They are the main ingredient of famous dishes, such as the rich French dish pommes Dauphinoise, in which layers of sliced potatoes are baked with garlic, milk, and cream.

How Are They Eaten?

Root vegetables are good in winter dishes such as soups and stews, where they act as thickeners and add flavor. Once cooked, they are often mashed to make a soft, tasty purée. Some root vegetables can be eaten raw. For example, carrots and beets can be grated into salads. Potatoes are boiled, roasted, baked, or sliced and fried to make french fries.

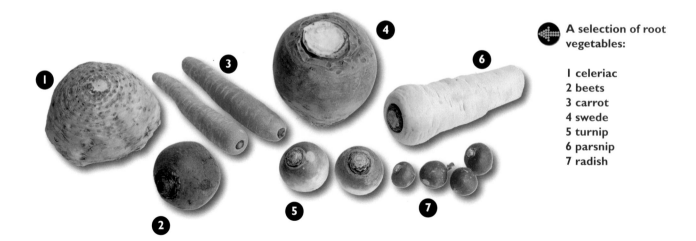

A selection of root vegetables:

1 celeriac
2 beets
3 carrot
4 swede
5 turnip
6 parsnip
7 radish

Choosing and Storing

Choose firm, well-shaped root vegetables and potatoes with no soft patches or sproutings. Potatoes should have no green patches on their skins. These vegetables have good keeping qualities and will last a week or two. Remove plastic packaging and store the vegetables loose, preferably in a vegetable rack in a cold, dark, airy place.

FOOD FACTS

Carrots and other yellow or orange foods contain a chemical called betacarotene. This works in the body like a vitamin, protecting it from harm.

Root vegetables keep well in the ground and some can even survive frost. Once pulled up, the stems and leaves are discarded and, in most root vegetables, the root is peeled and chopped.

Mashed Potatoes

SERVES: 2	PREPARATION TIME: 10 MINUTES	COOKING TIME: 20 MINUTES

Although this is a classic recipe for mashed potatoes, it can be used for root vegetables and other tubers or a combination of them.

Ingredients
2 medium potatoes
1 tablespoon butter
2 tablespoons milk
salt and pepper

1. Half fill a medium-sized saucepan with water. Heat the water to boiling. In the meantime, peel and wash the potatoes. Cut them into small pieces.

2. When the water is boiling rapidly, add the potatoes. Allow them to boil for about 20 minutes, until they are soft.

3. Use a colander to drain the potatoes, then put them back into the saucepan.

4. Add the butter and milk to the potatoes and mash with a potato masher or fork until the potatoes are smooth and soft. Season with salt and pepper to taste.

Scalloped Potatoes

SERVES: 4　　　　PREPARATION TIME: 20 MINUTES　　　　COOKING TIME: 30 MINUTES

This rich and creamy potato dish will go well with any meat recipe.

Ingredients
1½ lbs. (680 g) potatoes
1½ cups (350 ml) milk
1½ cups (350 ml) heavy cream
1 large garlic clove, peeled and
　finely chopped
salt and pepper
4 oz. (115 g) Gruyere cheese,
　grated

1. Preheat the oven to 400°F (200°C).

2. Peel and slice the potatoes thinly.

3. Put the milk and cream in a saucepan and heat to boiling.

4. Add the garlic, salt, and pepper to taste and simmer for 5 minutes.

5. Add the potato slices and stir gently. Simmer for about 10 minutes, until the potatoes are just tender.

6. Drain the potatoes in a colander, but catch the creamy milk in the saucepan or another bowl.

7. Cover the bottom of an ovenproof dish in potato slices. Sprinkle some of the grated Gruyere cheese over the layer of potatoes and add a little of the creamy milk. Repeat this until all the potatoes are in layers and you have used up two-thirds of the cheese.

8. Pour a little of the milk around the sides, just enough to slightly cover the potatoes. Sprinkle the last third of the cheese on top.

9. Bake in the oven for about 25 minutes until the cheese starts to bubble and turns golden brown.

10. Allow to stand for 10 minutes before serving.

COOK'S TIP

Aged Cheddar cheese can be used instead of the Gruyere.

Borscht

SERVES: 4	PREPARATION TIME: 20 MINUTES	COOKING TIME: 30 MINUTES

This traditional Polish soup is often served with dumplings.

Ingredients:

1 celeriac
1 carrot
1 onion
1 parsnip
3¾ cups (900 ml)
   water
2 beets
2 garlic cloves, peeled
   and finely chopped
juice of 1 lemon
1 teaspoon sugar
salt and pepper
sour cream, to serve

1. Peel and chop all the vegetables very finely.

2. Put the water in a saucepan and heat to boiling. Add the chopped vegetables and allow to boil for 20–30 minutes, until the vegetables are tender.

3. Without draining the vegetables, put them into a food processor and blend them to make a smooth purée.

4. Return the soup to the heat and add the garlic, lemon juice, and sugar and season to taste.

5. Ladle the soup into serving bowls. Serve with a dollop of sour cream.

Sweet Potato Soup

SERVES: 4	PREPARATION TIME: 20 MINUTES	COOKING TIME: 20 MINUTES

This soup is delicious served with heated naan or pita bread.

Ingredients

1 tablespoon
   sunflower oil
1 onion, peeled and
   finely chopped
1 garlic clove, peeled
   and finely chopped
1¾ lb. (800 g) sweet
   potatoes, grated
1 vegetable stock cube
   mixed with 1 quart water
¼ cup (50 ml) heavy cream
salt and pepper
fresh cilantro, to serve

1. Heat the oil in a large saucepan and fry the onion and garlic for 2–3 minutes.

2. Add the sweet potatoes and stock and heat to boiling. Allow to simmer for 15 minutes, until the potatoes are soft.

3. Remove from the heat and stir in the cream and seasoning to taste.

4. Use a food processor to make the soup smooth.

5. Sprinkle with fresh cilantro to serve.

Green Vegetables

Cabbage, broccoli, spinach, and cauliflower are some of the powerhouses of the vegetable kingdom. They are packed with vitamins and other disease-fighting nutrients.

Why Eat Greens?

Green vegetables are bursting with antioxidants, which help to prevent disease, and folic acid, which encourages healthy blood cells. Greens also contain minerals, including calcium, which helps to strengthen and repair bones and teeth; magnesium, which helps the body to release energy from food; and iron, which builds up red blood cells.

 A selection of green vegetables:

1 white cabbage	4 lettuce
2 spinach	5 broccoli
3 bok choi	6 cauliflower

FOOD FACTS

Dark, leafy spinach is packed with nutrients that benefit our digestive system, nerve function, skin, and sight. Kale and chard are other leafy greens that contain similar nutrients.

Where Are Greens Eaten?

Green vegetables are eaten wherever they will grow and are the basis of many famous dishes. In central and Eastern Europe, cabbage leaves are stuffed with rice, meat, and flavorings to make a hearty dish. Spinach is often served with eggs, for example in eggs Florentine, a well-known Italian dish. Elsewhere in southern Europe, peas and beans are often cooked in olive oil with garlic, onion, and or diced, cured ham. Bok choi and similar greens are essential ingredients in China and the Far East, where they are quickly wilted over the heat of a stove and served with stir-fries.

 Cooking broccoli in a steamer above a pan of boiling water helps to preserve its nutrients.

are all better than boiling. Some greens, such as escarole, can be baked in the oven. Cauliflower is often served with a cheese sauce. Most green vegetables are best served young, when they are sweet and tasty. The pods of peas and beans can then be eaten, too, and make delicious early summer soups.

How Are Greens Cooked?

Many green vegetables require very little cooking, which helps to preserve the nutrients they contain. Nutrients are easily destroyed in cooking, so it is good to eat greens raw in salads or to cook them briefly in as little liquid as possible. Steaming, stir-frying, and microwaving

Choosing and Storing Greens

Choose vegetables that are bright green, firm, and undamaged. Avoid greens that look limp or yellow. Greens are best stored in a cool, dark, dry place, preferably the refrigerator, for two to three days. Always eat them while they are fresh, as soon as possible after buying. All green vegetables need to be washed thoroughly before using.

Cooked Cabbage

SERVES: 2–3	PREPARATION TIME: 10 MINUTES	COOKING TIME: 10 MINUTES

This simple method of cooking can be used for most green vegetables.

Ingredients
I small cabbage, cut in half
I pat of butter
salt and pepper

1. Half fill a saucepan with water and heat to boiling.

2. In the meantime, cut out the middle stem of the cabbage since this is hard and will not cook or soften.

3. Chop the cabbage into strips and then again, so that the cabbage is in small pieces.

4. Wash the cabbage thoroughly. Shake off the water and add it to the boiling water. Allow it to cook for 10 minutes.

5. Use a colander to drain off the water and put the cabbage back in the saucepan.

6. Add the butter and salt and pepper to taste before serving.

COOK'S TIP

The water that is drained off the cabbage or other green vegetables contains a lot of Vitamin C and can be used to make gravy.

Eggs Florentine

Poached egg is perfectly teamed with the wilted spinach in this Italian dish.

Ingredients
2 oz. (50 g) fresh spinach
1 egg
1 teaspoon white vinegar
2 slices ciabatta bread
2 teaspoons olive oil
salt and pepper

1. Chop up the spinach and put it into a colander. Place the colander under cold water. Dry the spinach on a clean paper towel.

2. Crack the egg into a bowl.

3. Half fill a small saucepan with water and heat to boiling.

4. When the water is boiling, rapidly add the vinegar. Turn the water down to a simmer and stir it. When the water is swirling, add the egg and allow it poach for 2–3 minutes.

5. In the meantime, preheat the broiler if it is electric. Brush the bread with a little oil and place it under the broiler to toast.

6. Keeping an eye on the bread, place the spinach in a pan with the rest of the oil and cook over medium heat for 1 minute.

7. When the toast is ready, place it on a plate, then add the spinach and the egg on top of it.

8. Season with salt and pepper before serving.

COOK'S TIP

Whole-wheat bread can be used instead of ciabatta. It has more fiber than ciabatta so it is healthier.

Broccoli Beef Noodles

SERVES: 2 | **PREPARATION TIME: 15 MINUTES** | **COOKING TIME: 15 MINUTES**

This noodle dish is quick and easy to cook. If you prefer a milder flavor, you can leave out the red chili.

Ingredients
7.5 oz. (200 g) boneless sirloin
I bunch broccoli
I red chili, deseeded
I tablespoon oil
½ cup plus I tablespoon (150 ml) soy sauce
5 oz. (150 g) instant noodles

I. Slice beef into thin strips.

2. Chop broccoli and chili into bite-size pieces.

3. Heat the oil in a wok and add the beef and sauce. Fry until there is no pink meat left on the beef.

4. Add the broccoli and chili to the meat and stir well. Cook for 5 minutes, adding a little water if the mixture is dry.

5. Add the noodles and cook for 2–3 minutes. Serve piping hot.

Fava Beans and Ham

SERVES: 2 | **PREPARATION TIME: 15 MINUTES** | **COOKING TIME: 25 MINUTES**

This colorful dish makes a great side dish or main meal on its own.

Ingredients
2 lb. (900 g) fava beans
3½ tablespoons olive oil
4 oz. (115 g) Serrano ham, diced
2 garlic cloves, peeled and finely chopped
salt and pepper
I tablespoon chopped parsley, to serve

I. Shell and skin the beans, leaving a bright, green bean.

2. In a pan, heat the oil and fry the beans, ham, and garlic over high heat for 3–4 minutes.

3. Reduce the heat and cook for 20 minutes, until the beans are soft.

4. Season to taste and add the parsley before serving.

Vegetable Fruits

Vegetable fruits come in many different shapes, sizes, and colors, and are rich in tastes and textures. From avocados and squash to cucumbers and peppers, these fleshy foods are a good source of nutrition and provide us with a taste of summer all the year round.

Why Eat Vegetable Fruits?

These colorful vegetables are packed with goodness. For example, bell peppers contain large amounts of Vitamin C, which helps to heal wounds and prevent infection. Pumpkins and other squashes contain important minerals, such as potassium, which helps the heart, kidneys, and digestive system. Tomatoes contain a powerful antioxidant, known as lycopene, which helps to fight disease.

Where Are They Eaten?

Vegetable fruits are eaten all over the world. Peppers and chilies are popular in the Southwest and Mexico, where they put the heat into salsa.

In southern Europe, tomatoes, zucchini, eggplant, and bell peppers are used to make a stew known as ratatouille. Eggplants are important in Greece and the Middle East, where they are combined with minced lamb in moussaka. Pumpkins are associated with the United States. At Halloween, they are hollowed out and carved into lanterns. In the following month, they are made into a pie and served at Thanksgiving dinner.

FOOD FACTS

Red, yellow, and orange bell peppers all start out as green peppers but change color as they ripen. Chilies are a hot pepper and add heat to food.

A selection of vegetable fruits

1	bell peppers	5	zucchini
2	butternut squash	6	cherry tomatoes
3	acorn squash	7	chili
4	eggplant		

8	avocado
9	tomato
10	cucumber

How Are They Eaten?

Vegetable fruits are best broiled or roasted, which preserves and intensifies their flavor. Since many of these vegetables are large and sturdy, they can be hollowed out and filled with stuffings made of meat, rice, breadcrumbs, cheese, or herbs. Tomatoes can be simmered to make sauces for pasta, pizza, or meatballs. They can also be eaten raw in salads, along with cucumber, avocado, and bell peppers. Squashes are delicious roasted or stuffed or used to make soups, risottos, or pies.

Traditionally, pumpkins are carved into lanterns at Halloween and the flesh is used to make a pumpkin pie.

Ratatouille

SERVES: 2	PREPARATION TIME: 20 MINUTES	COOKING TIME: 30 MINUTES

This dish can be served as an accompaniment to a main meal or with warm bread as a main meal on its own.

Ingredients

2 eggplants, cut into cubes
2 zucchini, cut into slices
½ in. (1 cm) thick
2 tablespoons oil
1 onion, peeled and finely chopped
1 garlic clove, peeled and
finely chopped
14 oz. (400 g) can chopped
tomatoes
1 tablespoon fresh basil,
finely chopped
salt and pepper
bread, to serve

1. Place the eggplant cubes and zucchini in a colander. Sprinkle salt over them and cover them with a plate. Allow them to stand.

2. Heat the oil in a saucepan and fry the onion and garlic until the onion changes color but before it turns brown.

3. Rinse the eggplant and zucchini. Add them and the tomatoes to the saucepan and stir well. Allow to simmer for 30 minutes. Before serving, add the fresh basil.

COOK'S TIP

If you use fresh tomatoes instead of canned, you will need to skin them first (see page 47).

Pumpkin Pie

Pie pastry filled with mouthwatering pumpkin is perfect for Thanksgiving, served with whipped cream.

Ingredients

sunflower oil, for greasing
10 oz. (300 g) pumpkin flesh cut
    into cubes
1 egg
¼ cup (50 g) soft brown sugar
1 teaspoon cinnamon
½ cup (140 ml) heavy cream

For the pastry

¾ cup (100 g) all-purpose flour,
    plus extra for sprinkling
3½ tablespoons (50 g) butter
6 teaspoons cold water

1. Preheat the oven to 375°F (190°C). Lightly grease an 8 in. (20 cm) pie dish with oil.

2. Half fill a saucepan with water and heat to boiling. Add the chopped pumpkin and cook it for 10 minutes.

3. In the meantime, make the pastry. Rub the butter into the flour until it resembles fine breadcrumbs. (see page 47).

4. Use a metal spoon to stir in the cold water and mix well to make a soft dough.

5. Sprinkle flour on the work surface. Roll out the pastry so that it is large enough to line the bottom and sides of the pie dish. Set aside.

6. When the pumpkin is cooked, drain it in a colander and mash it as it as finely as possible.

7. Whisk the egg in a bowl and set it aside.

8. Place the sugar, cinnamon, and cream in a saucepan and allow it to simmer. Whisk it to mix well.

9. Pour the mixture over the egg and whisk well.

10. Add the pumpkin to the cream mixture and stir well.

11. Put the filling into the pastry and bake for 35–40 minutes until the center is slightly wobbly but the edges are puffed up.

COOK'S TIP

If you cannot find pumpkin, you could use butternut squash instead.

Caponata

SERVES: 2 | **PREPARATION TIME: 20 MINUTES** | **COOKING TIME: 40 MINUTES**

This traditional Sicilian dish can be served hot or cold.

Ingredients
2 eggplants, diced
1 onion
2 celery sticks
2 tablespoons sunflower oil
14 oz. (400 g) canned tomatoes
3.5 oz. (100 g) green olives
1 tablespoon capers
1 tablespoon sugar
2 tablespoons red wine
   vinegar
1 tablespoon parsley,
   chopped, to serve
salt and pepper

1. Sprinkle the eggplant with salt and allow to stand.

2. In the meantime, peel and chop the onion and celery.

3. Rinse the eggplant chunks and pat them dry with paper towel.

4. Heat the oil in a frying pan and fry the eggplant for about 10 minutes. Set them aside.

5. Fry the onions and celery until the onions are soft. Add the tomatoes and stir well. Add the olives and allow to simmer for 20 minutes.

6. Add the eggplant and capers to the pan and stir well. In a bowl, combine the sugar and vinegar and add them to the pan. Allow to cook for 10 minutes.

7. Sprinkle with the parsley and season to taste before serving.

Stuffed Peppers

SERVES: 2 | **PREPARATION TIME: 20 MINUTES** | **COOKING TIME: 10 MINUTES**

This quick and easy recipe is great as a lunchtime meal on a cold winter's day.

Ingredients
2 red bell peppers
½ cup (100 g) cooked rice
1 tablespoon basil pesto
4 pitted black
   olives, chopped
3.5 oz. (100 g) goat cheese,
   sliced

1. Cut the top off the peppers, then scoop out the seeds and pith. These insides can be thrown away.

2. Put the peppers on a plate, cut side up. Cook in a microwave oven on high for 5 minutes, until they have wilted and are soft.

3. While the peppers are cooking, mix the rice with the pesto, olives, and two-thirds of the cheese.

4. When the peppers are cooked, spoon the rice mixture into the peppers and top with the remaining cheese.

5. Return the peppers to the microwave oven and cook for a further 5 minutes on high so that the cheese melts.

Legumes

Healthy and versatile, legumes come in a variety of colors, shapes, and flavors. Easy to cook and tasty to eat, they add a filling texture and make many delicious dishes.

Fresh, Canned, or Frozen

This vegetable group includes fresh peas and beans, which grow in long, green pods. If the pods are thoroughly dried, their round or oval seeds can be shelled and stored for future use.

Why Eat Legumes?

Legumes are rich in proteins and, when eaten with grains, form the same high-quality proteins as those found in meat and fish. This makes legumes invaluable for vegetarians. They are a good source of fiber, carbohydrates, vitamins, and minerals, including iron. Because legumes are complex carbohydrates, they release their sugars gradually, which makes them useful for diabetics, who need to keep their sugar levels constant. With the exception of soybeans, legumes are low in fat.

How Are Legumes Eaten?

Peas and beans can be eaten in different ways. Some peas are removed from the pod, while others, such as snow peas and snap peas, are eaten pod and all. They are very good in stir-fries. Fava beans are removed from the pod, but with most beans the pod is eaten, too—either whole or cut into slices.

Legumes can be eaten as a side vegetable and they are often combined with other foods in soups, stews, casseroles, and curries.

Fresh peas and beans (top) are delicious in season. Their dried seeds (middle) are very hard. Dried legumes need to be soaked and cooked, but are also available canned (bottom).

In India, dhal, made from lentils, is a staple food. In the Middle East, people enjoy dipping warm pita bread in a purée of chickpeas, olive oil, and garlic, which is known as hummus.

Soybeans

Soybeans are rich in fats and contain twice as much protein as other legumes. They can be processed to make soy milk and tofu, which is a firm curd that is widely used in Asian food.

Choosing and Storing Legumes

Choose legumes with a deep, glossy color, avoiding any that look faded. They should be stored in a refrigerator. Legumes need to be stored in an airtight container away from heat, light, and moisture. They will keep fresh for up to a year. Many legumes need to be soaked overnight, and then boiled for up to an hour or more. Fortunately, many legumes are available canned and ready to eat.

Tofu, also known as bean curd, is made from soy milk, which is produced from soybeans. Tofu has very little taste of its own but absorbs the flavors of other ingredients.

Hummus

SERVES: 2	PREPARATION TIME: 10 MINUTES	COOKING TIME: NO COOKING

This Middle Eastern dip is often served with warmed pita bread and black olives. The chickpeas are a good source of protein.

Ingredients

14 oz. (400 g) can chickpeas, rinsed
   and drained
1 garlic clove, peeled and
   finely chopped
1 tablespoon lemon juice
1 tablespoon olive oil
1 tablespoon tahini
   (sesame seed paste)
salt and pepper
pita bread and olives,
   to serve

1. Put all the ingredients, except the salt and pepper, in a large bowl or food processor and mash or blend to a smooth consistency.

2. Add salt and pepper to taste. Blend again. Serve with warm pita bread and olives.

COOK'S TIP

Dried chickpeas can be used, but they need to be soaked overnight and boiled for about two hours before using.

Lentil Dhal

This traditional Indian dish is delicious served with mango chutney.

Ingredients

4 tablespoons sunflower oil
1 teaspoon cumin seeds
1 teaspoon cilantro seeds
¼ teaspoon turmeric
1 onion, peeled and finely chopped
1 garlic clove, peeled and finely chopped
1 cup (200 g) red lentils
1 quart (1 liter) water
5 oz. (150 g) green beans
4 tomatoes

1. Heat half of the oil in a large saucepan. Add the spice seeds and fry them for 2 minutes.

2. Remove the spices from the pan and put them in a mortar and pestle. Crush them.

3. Using the same pan, heat the remaining oil and fry the onion and garlic for 2 minutes.

4. Add the spices and stir well. Cook for another 2 minutes.

5. Add the lentils and water. Heat to boiling, then allow to simmer for 40 minutes. If the mixture becomes dry, add more water.

6. In the meantime, prepare the green beans by trimming the ends and cutting them into pieces ¼ in. (5 mm) long.

7. Cut the tomatoes into small, bite-sized pieces.

8. When the lentils are soft, add the beans and tomatoes and cook the dhal for a further 5 minutes.

COOK'S TIP

Add a fresh chili or chili powder for some heat.

Tuna and Bean Salad

SERVES: 2	PREPARATION TIME: 20 MINUTES	COOKING TIME: NO COOKING

This salad is packed with lots of beans, giving you all the protein you need.

Ingredients

4 oz. (100 g) frozen green beans, thawed
6 oz. (185 g) can tuna, drained
14 oz. (400 g) can cannelloni beans, drained
1 red onion, peeled and chopped
1 tablespoon olive oil
1 tablespoon lemon juice
2 garlic cloves, peeled and chopped
2 tablespoons Parmesan cheese, grated
salt and pepper

1. Put all the ingredients in a large bowl. Season to taste and mix well.

2. Cover with plastic wrap and refrigerate for about an hour before serving.

COOK'S TIP

Fresh green beans can be used, but they need to be blanched (see page 47) before adding them to the other ingredients.

Minestrone Soup

SERVES: 4–6	PREPARATION TIME: 25 MINUTES	COOKING TIME: 1 HOUR 15 MINUTES

This hearty Italian soup makes an ideal meal on a cold winter's day.

Ingredients

1 tablespoon oil
1 onion, peeled and chopped
1 garlic clove, peeled and finely chopped
2 quarts (2 liters) water
2 oz. (50 g) navy beans
2 carrots, peeled and diced
2 celery sticks, chopped
2 potatoes, peeled and diced
2 zucchini, chopped
4 tomatoes, chopped
2 oz. (50 g) small macaroni
1 tablespoon chopped parsley
2 oz. (50 g) shavings Parmesan cheese

1. Heat the oil in a large saucepan. Fry the onion and garlic until they change color, but not until they are brown.

2. Add the water and navy beans and heat to boiling. Allow to simmer for 15 minutes.

3. Add all the other vegetables, bring the mixture back to boiling, and then simmer for 45 minutes.

4. Add the macaroni and cook for a further 15 minutes.

5. Stir in the parsley and serve with the shavings of Parmesan cheese.

Orchard Fruits

There is an old saying that "an apple a day keeps the doctor away." The same could be said of the other orchard fruits, such as plums and pears. These healthy foods are good for snacking and are also used in drinks and desserts.

What Are Orchard Fruits?

Orchard fruits include apples, apricots, cherries, pears, plums, quinces, peaches, and nectarines. Each group includes many different varieties. In the United States alone, for example, there are nearly 2,500 different varieties of apple, ranging from small, sweet dessert apples to larger, sharper cooking varieties.

Why Eat Orchard Fruits?

Orchard fruits are an important part of a healthy diet. They are packed with antioxidants—vitamins that destroy harmful substances in the body that can build up and cause disease. They also contain important minerals and are fat free. Eaten with their skins on, they are a great source of fiber, which is important to keep our digestion working properly.

How Do They Grow?

Apples, pears, and plums grow in cool, temperate places, while apricots, peaches, and nectarines require a warmer climate. In the spring, the fruit trees are covered in blossoms, which attracts bees and other insects. As the insects feed on the sweet-smelling nectar, they pollinate the flowers, enabling the fruits to develop. Throughout the summer, the fruit swells and ripens. The earliest varieties are harvested in midsummer; the latest in early fall. There are dozens of different ways to make use of the seasonal harvest.

Apples, pears, and plums have sweet, juicy flesh, which surrounds the seeds or "pits." All of these fruits make healthy snacks.

How Are They Eaten?

Most orchard fruits are delicious eaten raw. Apples are particularly good for snacking because they are robust and less likely to bruise when carried around. The fruit can also be eaten chopped in granola or cereals or they can be added to salads.

FOOD FACTS

To meet one of your five-a-day portions, just eat one apple, peach or pear, two plums, three apricots, or a small bowl of cherries.

Orchard fruits can also be cooked. This softens them and changes their flavor. They can be stewed and served in pies, cobblers, and crumbles, added to cakes, or simply baked. Apples appear in many famous recipes such as apple pie or Dutch apple cake. Pears may be stewed in wine or cooked and coated with chocolate sauce, as in the French dessert Belle Helene. Baked peaches are used in Peach Melba, alongside ice cream and raspberry sauce.

Processing the Fruit

Most orchard fruits can be turned into juices, ciders, and other drinks or preserved in chutneys. The fruit can also be preserved by drying. Dried apricots make a tasty snack and are especially good when soaked and cooked, and then served in a syrup. Dried cherries are used in cakes and pies.

Unlike most fruit, pears need to be harvested before they are ready to eat, usually in late summer. The fruit ripens about one to two weeks after picking.

Orchard Fruit Crumble

SERVES: 2	PREPARATION TIME: 30 MINUTES	COOKING TIME: 20 MINUTES

This twist on apple crumble uses pears and plums. It can be served with cream, ice cream, or custard.

Ingredients
3½ tablespoons (50 g) margarine or butter
¾ cup (100 g) all-purpose flour
¼ cup (50 g) sugar
2 oz. (50 g) rolled oats
1 pear, peeled
1 plum
2 tablespoons water

1. Preheat the oven to 350°F (180°C).

2. Rub the margarine or butter into the flour until the mixture resembles fine breadcrumbs (see page 47).

3. Stir in the sugar and oats.

4. Cut the fruit into small cubes so that they resemble dice. Place them in a small ovenproof dish and add the water.

5. Sprinkle the crumble mixture over the top and bake in the oven for 20 minutes.

Dutch Apple Cake

SERVES: 2	PREPARATION TIME: 30 MINUTES	COOKING TIME: 20 MINUTES

This cake makes a perfect treat when served with fresh cream.

Ingredients

4½ tablespoons (65 g) butter, plus extra for greasing
1½ cups (175 g) superfine sugar
1 medium egg
1 cup (125 g) all-purpose flour
½ teaspoon baking powder
1 teaspoon ground nutmeg
12 oz. (350 g) apples, diced
whipped cream, to serve

1. Preheat the oven to 350°F (180°C).

2. Cream the butter and sugar.

3. Add the egg and mix well.

4. Add the flour, baking powder, and nutmeg and stir to make a smooth batter.

5. Add the apples and mix well.

6. Pour the mixture into an 7 in. (18 cm) greased can. Bake for 1 hour and 15 minutes.

7. Lower the temperature to 300°F (150°C) and bake for 20 minutes. Remove from the oven and allow to cool on a wire rack before serving.

Peach Melba

SERVES: 2	PREPARATION TIME: 30 MINUTES	COOKING TIME: 5 MINUTES

This recipe is named after the Australian opera singer Dame Nellie Melba and is a favorite with adults and children alike.

Ingredients

2 egg whites
1 tablespoon superfine sugar
½ cup (125 ml) heavy cream
1 drop vanilla extract
1 peach, pit removed

1. Whisk the egg whites until they form soft peaks. Add the sugar and whisk until stiff peaks form.

2. Place the cream and vanilla extract in a separate bowl and whisk until thick.

3. Divide the cream into two servings and put a peach half on top of each one.

4. Spoon the egg whites into a piping bag and pipe them over each peach half in a spiral shape.

5. Carefully use a chef's torch to glaze the meringue until golden brown. Serve immediately.

COOK'S TIP

If you over-whisk the cream, clots will form and it will look like cottage cheese.

Poached Pears with Chocolate Sauce

SERVES: 2 | **PREPARATION TIME: 30 MINUTES** | **COOKING TIME: 30 MINUTES**

This traditional French recipe is called Poires Belle Helene. It can be served with a scoop of rich vanilla ice cream.

Ingredients
2 pears, peeled but with the stalk
  in tact
1½ cups (375 ml) water
1¾ cups (375 g) sugar

For the chocolate sauce
1 cup (250 ml) heavy cream
10 oz. (300 g) milk chocolate,
  broken into pieces

1. Cut the pears in half lengthwise and remove the core. Slice the bottom off each half to make a flat base.

2. Place the pears upright in a pan with the water and sugar and cook for 20 minutes, until tender but firm enough to stand up.

3. In the meantime, to make the chocolate sauce, put the cream in saucepan over low heat. Add the chocolate pieces and heat until the chocolate has melted. Stir well.

4. Remove the pears from the pan, keeping the syrup. Place each one standing up on a serving plate.

5. Add a tablespoon of the syrup to the chocolate sauce and stir well.

6. Pour the chocolate sauce over the pears and serve.

COOK'S TIP

Use a potato peeler to peel the pears.

Berries and Currants

Strawberries, raspberries, black currants—we associate these sweet, deep-colored fruit with warm summer days. Though many of them are delicious raw, they can also be used to make mouth-watering desserts.

 Berries come in different sizes and colors. From left to right: blackberries, strawberries, blueberries, raspberries.

What Are Berries and Currants?

Berries and currants are the fruit of certain flowering plants, which have been bred to produce tasty fruit. Berry fruits grown in gardens and on farms include strawberries, raspberries, loganberries, tayberries, cranberries, gooseberries, and blueberries. Raspberries are grown on tall canes, and strawberries are grown in beds on the ground, surrounded by straw to keep the fruit clean. Blueberries and cranberries grow in cooler places and prefer boggy ground. Currants are small and round in shape and can be black, red, or white. These fruits come in many different varieties, each one slightly different in its appearance, flavor, or fruiting time. Currants grow best in full sun.

Why Eat Berries and Currants?

Berry fruits are often called "super foods" because of their nutritional goodness. Like many other colorful foods, they are rich in antioxidants that destroy harmful substances in the body, which can build up and cause cancers. The fruits are particularly rich in Vitamin C, boosting the immune system in the fight against disease. Aside from their nutritional content, the soft fruits are easy to serve and require little preparation. Best of all, they taste delicious.

FOOD FACTS

One 5 fl. oz. (150 ml) serving of cranberry juice contains many disease-busting nutrients, including the recommended daily requirement for Vitamin C. Doctors routinely recommend the juice to people who suffer from bladder infections.

Choosing and Storing Berry Fruit

Berries and currants are highly perishable, so they need to be used within a few days of purchase. Choose perfect-looking fruit and store in the refrigerator. Always wash the fruit before eating or using it in recipes.

How Are They Eaten?

All berries can be eaten raw, added to cereals and smoothies, or served with yogurt, ice cream, or cream. In the Australian dessert, raspberry pavlova, fresh raspberries are served on a thick meringue base, and strawberries and cream are a traditional English favourite.

Currants are too sharp for eating raw and should be gently cooked and sweetened with sugar. They can then be used in cobblers and pies, or puréed and sieved to make sauces and coulis. At the height of the season, all of these fruits can be preserved by boiling with sugar to make preserves and jellies. Some are used to make juices or liqueurs. Black currant juice is popular in the UK, while in France, the fruit is used to create cassis, a popular liqueur.

Strawberries are grown in beds on sunny, well-drained soil. In late spring, straw is laid under the plants to prevent the growing fruit from touching the ground. Strawberries need to be picked as soon as they are ripe to prevent them from rotting.

Summer Bread Pudding

SERVES: 4 | PREPARATION TIME: 30 MINUTES | CHILLING TIME: OVERNIGHT

This summer pudding uses a mix of different berries to create a mouth-watering dessert.

Ingredients
2 tablespoons water
¾ cup (150 g) sugar
1 lb. (450 g) mixed berries
4–6 slices of white bread
whipped cream, to serve

1. Put the water and sugar in a saucepan and heat to boiling.

2. Add the fruits and stew gently until they are soft but still have their shape.

3. Cut the crusts off the bread. Line a 1 quart (1 liter) bowl with the bread.

4. Pour in the fruit and cover with more slices of bread.

5. Place a saucer with a weight on it on top of the pudding and leave it overnight in the refrigerator.

6. Turn out the pudding and serve with cream.

COOK'S TIP
You can make miniature summer puddings by using small ramekins instead of one big bowl.

Strawberry Foam

SERVES: 2 | PREPARATION TIME: 30 MINUTES | COOKING TIME: NO COOKING

This light and fluffy strawberry mousse is perfect on a hot summer's day.

Ingredients
8 oz. (225 g) ripe strawberries
1 egg white
¾ cup (75 g) confectioners' sugar

1. Remove the stems from the strawberries and put them in a large mixing bowl.

2. Reserve two strawberries for serving. Mash the remaining strawberries until smooth.

3. Add the egg white and confectioners' sugar to the strawberries. Whisk for about 10 minutes until the mixture is thick and frothy.

4. Pile the mixture into glasses and chill until ready to serve. Before serving, garnish with the two reserved strawberries.

Raspberry Pavlova

SERVES: 6	PREPARATION TIME: 40 MINUTES	COOKING TIME: 1 HOUR

This delicious berry dessert never fails to impress people.

Ingredients
3 egg whites
¾ cup (175 g) superfine sugar
1 teaspoon cornstarch
½ teaspoon vinegar
1¼ cups (285 ml) heavy cream
8 oz. (250 g) fresh raspberries
confectioners' sugar, to serve

1. Preheat the oven to 300°F (150°C).

2. Draw a circle 7 in. (18 cm) in diameter on baking paper and place the paper on a baking tray.

3. Whisk the egg whites until they are stiff. Add the sugar a little at a time and whisk.

4. Add the cornstarch and vinegar and whisk until the egg whites are very stiff and shiny. You should be able to turn the bowl upside down without the mixture moving.

5. Spread the meringue mixture over the circle of waxed paper and bake for about 1 hour until the meringue is firm.

6. When baked, remove the meringue from the oven and allow to cool before transferring it to a flat plate.

7. Whisk the cream until thick and pile it on top of the meringue. Arrange the raspberries on top of the meringue, dust with confectioners' sugar and serve.

COOK'S TIP

You could use strawberries, blackberries, blueberries, or a combination of them instead of raspberries.

Citrus Fruits

Most of us enjoy a glass of orange juice or grapefruit juice to start the day. Citrus fruits are full of tangy juice with a delicious fruity flavor. They help to cleanse the system and give us some get-up-and-go!

What Are Citrus Fruits?

Citrus fruits include oranges, lemons, limes, grapefruit, mandarin oranges, pomelos, and tangerines. The fruit grows in segments with a thin, edible skin, called the pith. Each fruit is surrounded by a thick peel, which has to be removed before eating. The fruits grow in groves or orchards in places with a subtropical climate, such as California, Brazil, Spain, and South Africa. The fruits develop in the summer, ripen in the fall, and are harvested during the winter.

Why Eat Citrus Fruits?

Citrus fruits are extremely healthy and contain large amounts of fiber, minerals, and vitamins, notably Vitamin C. Their high dosage of Vitamin C means that eating them regularly can help to prevent colds and flu. The fruits are all acidic and are excellent at helping to get rid of toxins (the harmful chemicals that our bodies absorb from fumes, cleaning products, fertilizers, and pesticides). Toxins are believed to contribute to disease and can cause a lack of energy.

Citrus fruits are bursting with juice. Clockwise from top left: lime, grapefruit, lemon, orange.

FOOD FACTS

A glass of orange juice counts as only one portion of fruit. Eating whole fruit is much more nutritious.

FOOD FACTS

A mandarin orange is a type of small citrus fruit with a loose, yellow-orange skin. A tangerine is a citrus fruit with a loose, deep red-orange skin. A clementine is a seedless tangerine and also has a deep orange-red skin.

How Are They Eaten?

Oranges, mandarin oranges, clementines, and tangerines are all sweet enough to be eaten raw. They are portable and easy to peel. An orange flavor goes well with chocolate and so orange juice or zest is often added to cakes and desserts. Grapefruits are often eaten before a meal, usually breakfast, because their sharper juice cleanses the palate and stimulates the body's digestive juices. Lemons are mainly used in cooking and to make popular desserts such as lemon sorbet

and lemon meringue pie. In Morocco, they are preserved in salt to add flavor to local stews called tagines. Lime, which is both tangy and sweet, is widely used in Thai cooking, which is full of lively flavors.

Processing the Fruit

Much of the world's vast citrus harvest is turned into juice and shipped around the world. The juice is also added to ices, lemonade, and fruit punches. Lemons can be used to make lemon curd, and sour oranges (known as Seville oranges) are boiled with sugar to make marmalade—a jellylike staple of the traditional British breakfast.

Like all citrus fruits, oranges are green at first but change color as they ripen. Once it is ripe, the fruit can stay on the tree for weeks or months before it is picked.

Lemon Sorbet

Refreshing, tangy, and ice-cold, lemon sorbet makes a great alternative to ice cream after a main meal.

Ingredients
½ cup (100 g) superfine sugar
1¼ cups (300 ml) water
juice of 3 lemons
zest of one lemon
2 egg whites

1. Put the sugar and water in a saucepan over low heat. Heat to boiling and allow to simmer for 10 minutes.

2. Add a tablespoon of the lemon juice and stir.

3. Put the zest in a bowl and pour over the hot syrup. Allow to cool.

4. When cold, add the remaining lemon juice and mix well.

5. Put the mixture in a sealed tub in the freezer until it is a slushy consistency.

6. Whisk the egg whites until they are stiff, then fold them into the lemon slush.

7. Put the sorbet back in the freezer until the ice sets. Serve in tall glasses or bowls.

COOK'S TIP

Use oranges or grapefruit instead of lemons—or a combination of all three for a zesty sorbet.

Mandarin Orange Cupcakes

SERVES: 12 | **PREPARATION TIME: 30 MINUTES** | **COOKING TIME: 20 MINUTES**

The light sponge and sweet mandarin orange of this recipe combine to make delicious cupcakes.

Ingredients

2 mandarin oranges
¾ cup (100 g) all-purpose flour
½ teaspoon baking powder
½ cup (100 g) superfine sugar
7 tablespoons (100 g) margarine
2 eggs
confectioners' sugar, to serve

1. Preheat the oven to 350°F (180°C). Line a 12-hole muffin pan with baking cups.

2. Peel the mandarin oranges and chop them into very small pieces. Set aside.

3. Place the flour, baking powder, sugar, margarine, and eggs in a bowl and mix together until the mixture makes a creamy mousse.

4. Add the mandarin orange pieces and mix well.

5. Spread the batter out evenly into the cupcake cases.

6. Bake for 20 minutes. Remove from the oven and allow to cool on a wire rack before dusting with confectioners' sugar.

COOK'S TIP

You can tell when the cupcakes are ready because the cake will bounce back when you touch it.

Citrus Wake Up

SERVES: 4 | **PREPARATION TIME: 30 MINUTES** | **COOKING TIME: NO COOKING**

This drink is packed with Vitamin C and so it is a great, healthy way to start your day.

Ingredients

4 oranges
1 red grapefruit
1 lemon
1 lime
zest of one lime
½ cup (120 ml) water
1 tablespoon superfine sugar
2 tablespoons fresh mint, shredded
lemon or orange slices, to serve

1. Cut the oranges, grapefruit, lemon, and lime in half around the center.

2. Use a hand juicer to squeeze out all the juice from the fruits.

3. Combine the juices with the lime zest, water, sugar, and mint.

4. Pour the juice into glasses. Serve with a slice of lemon or orange.

Tropical Fruits

Many of the most delicious fruits grow in the tropics—the warmest, wettest parts of the world. Due to air-freighting, they are now transported all over the world and people who live in cooler places can enjoy them, too.

A plateful of tropical flavor. Clockwise from left: passion fruit, papaya, mango, pineapple, lychee, banana.

How and Where Do They Grow?

Bananas and pineapples are the fruit of herbaceous plants, which are grown throughout the tropics. Lychees, mangoes, and papayas grow on trees. Lychees, which are called the cherries of Asia, are found in China, Vietnam, Pakistan, India, Bangladesh, and other parts of Asia. Passion fruit and kiwi fruit grow on woody vines. Passion fruit is found through the topics but particularly in South America and South Africa, and kiwi fruit, which originated in China, are now also grown in New Zealand and Italy.

Eating Tropical Fruits

Most tropical fruits have a delicious aroma and flavor and they make excellent desserts. They are nutritional powerhouses, packed with vitamins and minerals, such as iron and potassium, and adding plenty of fiber to our diet. A single mango provides 40 percent of our daily fiber requirement. Many of the tropical fruits contain powerful enzymes. These are chemicals that aid digestion and are particularly good at breaking down proteins such as cheese or meat. This is why pineapple has traditionally been served with ham.

How Are They Eaten?

All tropical fruits can be eaten raw, either on their own or mixed with other ingredients—for example, in a fruit salad or as a topping on meringue. They are great thirst quenchers and their strong flavors and bright colors makes them excellent for juices or smoothies.

Papayas may be served chilled as an appetizer with a squeeze of lime juice. Mangoes can also be cooked and served in dips, such as salsas, and chutneys. Many tropical fruits are preserved by canning and some are also available dried. However, they are much more nutritious if eaten fresh.

Choosing and Storing Tropical Fruits

Choose undamaged fruit and allow it to ripen at room temperature. Never put bananas in the refrigerator or they will rot from the inside.

FOOD FACTS

Bananas are the world's most popular fruit. Many varieties are eaten raw but some, called plantains, must be cooked. The plantain is a staple food in many tropical countries, taking the role of the potato in cooler regions.

Pineapples and bananas are on many people's weekly shopping list. Air transportation has made tropical fruits available in supermarkets around the world.

Pineapple and Ham Pizza

SERVES: 2   **PREPARATION TIME: 40 MINUTES**   **COOKING TIME: 20–30 MINUTES**

Sometimes called a Hawaiian pizza, this combination of ham and pineapple makes a great pizza topping.

Ingredients

1½ cups (200 g) flour, plus extra for dusting
1½ teaspoons dried yeast
1 teaspoon salt
½ cup (125 ml) warm water
7 oz. (200 g) can pineapple cubes
2 fresh tomatoes
2 oz. (50 g) Cheddar cheese
2 oz. (50 g) mozzarella cheese
2 oz. (50 g) cooked ham
1 tablespoon vegetable oil

1. Put the flour, yeast, and salt into a bowl. Add the warm water and mix to form a soft dough.

2. Place the dough on a lightly floured work surface and knead (see page 47) for 10 minutes.

3. Preheat the oven to 400°F (200°C).

4. Stretch the dough into a circle and place it on a baking sheet. Cover it with plastic wrap and allow it to rise for 20 minutes.

5. In the meantime, drain the can of pineapple cubes.

6. Cut the tomatoes into slices about ¼ in. (5 mm) thick. Grate all the cheese and tear the ham into bite-sized pieces.

7. Brush the pizza base with the oil and bake it on its own for 5 minutes.

8. When the base it ready, take it out of the oven and place the tomato slices on top of it. Then add the ham, cheese, and pineapple cubes.

9. Bake for 20 minutes until the base is crispy and the topping is golden brown.

Banana and Mango Smoothie

SERVES: 2	PREPARATION TIME: 20 MINUTES	COOKING TIME: NO COOKING

Tropical fruits work really well in smoothies and fruit juices. This drink combines two of the world's favorite fruits.

Ingredients
½ ripe mango
1 banana
½ cup (120 ml) milk
½ cup (120 ml) orange juice
2 teaspoons lime juice
1 tablespoon superfine sugar
2 heaping teaspoons vanilla frozen yogurt

1. Peel the mango and cut the flesh away from the pit. Dice the flesh.

2. Peel and dice the banana.

3. Put the mango and banana in a blender and add all the other ingredients. Blend for about 30 seconds to make a light and frothy drink.

4. Pour the smoothie into tall glasses and serve immediately.

Far Eastern Fruit Salad

SERVES: 4	PREPARATION TIME: 15–20 MINUTES	COOKING TIME: NO COOKING

You can use any tropical fruit in this salad. Try adding kiwi fruit instead of the grapes.

Ingredients
15 oz. (425 g) can lychees in syrup
3 pieces stem ginger (bottled ginger) plus 2 tablespoons of the syrup
zest and juice of one lime
2 oranges, cut into small pieces
1 mango, peeled and diced
7.5 oz. (200 g) black or red grapes
1 banana

1. Drain the lychees over a bowl.

2. Discard half the syrup, then add the lychees to the bowl.

3. Add all the other ingredients and stir well.

4. Spoon into bowls and serve.

COOK'S TIP

If you are not serving the salad right away, do not add the bananas as they will turn brown. Add them just before serving instead.

Glossary

antioxidant — a type of vitamin substance believed to protect body cells from damage and aging

betacarotene — one of a group of yellow and red pigments contained in some plants

blanching — to precook something for a very short time

carbohydrate — a nutrient that gives the body energy

chutney — a thick, spicy accompaniment to food, made of chopped fruits or vegetables cooked in vinegar and sugar with spices

coulis — a fruit purée thin enough to pour

crouton — a small, crisp piece of toasted or fried bread, usually eaten in soups or salads, such as Caesar salad

diabetes — a medical condition in which the body is unable to control the level of sugar in the blood

enzyme — a chemical agent that changes food into substances that our bodies can absorb

feta cheese — a firm Greek cheese with a tangy flavor made from sheep's milk

fiber — the bulky part of food, known as roughage, that is needed for digestion

grain — the seed that comes from edible grasses, such as rice and oats

iron — a mineral found in certain foods, such as green, leafy vegetables, legumes, and meat, which our body needs to be healthy

knead — to make dough soft and elastic by folding and pummeling

legume — the seed or pod of a plant of the pea or bean family

lycopene — a red pigment found in tomatoes and other foods that works as an antioxidant in the body

magnesium — a mineral found in certain foods, such as green vegetables, that our body needs in order to be healthy

mineral — a substance, such as iron, that is found in the soil and the foods we eat

nutrient — any part of a food that gives the body energy or the goodness it needs to grow

parboiled — when something is boiled before roasting or frying

perishable — likely to rot or go bad quickly

pesticide — a chemical substance that is used to kill pests or weeds. Washing fruit and vegetables is important because it removes pesticides

preserve — to keep something in its existing state, for example, by eating fruit and vegetables raw, you preserve their vitamin and minerals

potassium — a mineral found in certain foods, such as squashes and bananas, which our body needs in order to be healthy

purée — food that has been cooked then mashed or blended until it makes a smooth, thick pulp

risotto — an Italian dish of rice cooked in stock with vegetables, meat, or fish

salsa — a spicy sauce of chopped, usually uncooked vegetables such as onion, tomatoes, chili, and bell peppers

saturated fat — a type of fat that is harmful to the body because it builds up in the arteries and causes heart disease

staple — basic, necessary

subtropical — belonging to the area north and south of the Tropics; the climate is generally hot and humid in summer and mild or cool in winter

temperate — mild

toxin — a poisonous substance

vitamin — a special substance found in food, which the body needs in tiny amounts to stay healthy

Food Safety

Sticking to some simple rules can help you avoid food poisoning and other kitchen dangers.

1. Clean all your work surfaces before you start cooking.

2. If you have long hair, tie it back away from your face.

3. To avoid a serious injury, always wear shoes in the kitchen.

4. Wash your hands well with soap and warm water before you start to cook. Wash them after handling any raw meat, poultry, or fish.

5. Read through the recipe you are cooking before you start. Check that you have all the equipment and ingredients that you will need.

6. Check the use-by dates on all food.

7. Wash all fruit and vegetables under cold running water.

8. When preparing food, keep it out of the refrigerator for the shortest time possible. Generally, you should not leave food out for longer than 2 hours.

9. Use a different cutting board and knife to prepare meat, chicken, and fish from the one you use for preparing fruit and vegetables.

10. Never serve undercooked food, ensure that any meat, fish, and chicken is cooked all the way through.

11. Replace used dish towels regularly with clean, dry ones to avoid the spreading of bacteria.

 KNOW YOUR FOOD

Useful Information
These abbreviations have been used:
lb.—pound   **oz.**—ounce
ml—milliliter   **g**—gram
cm—centimeter   **mm**—millimeter

1 teaspoon = 5 milliliters
1 tablespoon = 15 milliliters

All eggs are medium unless stated.

Cooking temperatures:
To figure out where the stove dial needs to be for high, medium, and low heat, count the marks on the dial and divide them by three. The top few are high, the bottom few are low, and the in-between ones are medium.

Useful Techniques

Dicing
Cut the fruit or vegetable intro strips about ½ in. (1 cm) wide, then chop the vegetable to give you cubes about ½ in. (1 cm) in size.

Blanching
Place the vegetables in a saucepan with just enough boiling water to cover them. Keep them in the water for the required time, which will vary depending on the recipe.

Rubbing In
Use your fingertips to "squash" the butter into the flour. Continue to do this until the flour resembles bread crumbs.

Mashing
Use either a fork or a masher to press down to squash the fruit or vegetable. Continue to do this until there are no lumps left.

Peeling Tomatoes
Use a sharp knife to make a cross at the bottom of the tomato. Cover the tomato with boiling water and leave to stand for 3 minutes before removing. The skin should peel back from the cross.

Poaching Eggs
Put water in a saucepan to boil. When it is boiling, stir it to create a "whirlpool." Crack the egg into the water and allow it to boil for the desired length of time.

Kneading
Press down on the dough with the palm of your hand, then fold the dough over itself and press down again. Continue to do this until the dough is soft and elastic.

Index

Further Reading

Body Fuel For Healthy Bodies: Grains, Fruits, Vegetables, and Legumes
by Trisha Sertori (Marshall Cavendish Children's Books, 2008)

Healthy Eating: Fruits and Vegetables
by Susan Martineau (Smart Apple Media, 2009)

Yum: Your Ultimate Manual for Good Nutrition
by Daina Kalnins (Lobster Press, 2008)

Web Sites

Due to the changing nature of Internet links, Rosen Publishing has developed an online list of Web sites related to the subject of this book. This site is regularly updated. Please use this link to access this list: http://www.rosenlinks.com/cook/cfv